Information Security
For
The Little Guy

Information Security
For
The Little Guy

Joseph M Hoffman

iUniverse, Inc.
New York Lincoln Shanghai

Information Security For The Little Guy

iUniverse books may be ordered through booksellers or by contacting:

iUniverse
2021 Pine Lake Road, Suite 100
Lincoln, NE 68512
www.iuniverse.com
1-800-Authors (1-800-288-4677)

ISBN-13: 978-0-595-38624-6 (pbk)
ISBN-13: 978-0-595-83004-6 (ebk)
ISBN-10: 0-595-38624-5 (pbk)
ISBN-10: 0-595-83004-8 (ebk)

Printed in the United States of America

Contents

Introduction

Being secure in an insecure world is a tough nut to crack. There are so many ways that our personal information can be stolen and duplicated today it is a very serious situation and should be taken very seriously.

From our surfing the Internet to just the simplicity of speaking on a cell phone to our friends can cause an invasion of privacy or worse the capture of personal information that can be reused in order to obtain our bank accounts, identity, and all our financial data to the point of causing bankruptcy and or defamation of our good name in society today.

The following chapters of information are an attempt to make the individual aware of the threats and precautions that can be taken in a formal specific way that any major corporation in the market place would as they do today. Joseph M. Hoffman is a Certified Information Systems Security Professional (CISSP) and has worked as a Security Consultant with many multi-national corporations and has organized this book in a fashion as it relates to the individual or average Joe as they say to help the individual combat against the many threats that our fast paced world of electronics has presented us with. In honor of my wife and life long love I dedicate this book, Kim Hoffman.

1

Personal Security Management Practices

For most people, the most serious obstacle to personal safety is an attitude of complacency or fatalism. "It can't happen to me" and "if it's going to happen, it's going to happen" is dangerous thinking.

Recent political events throughout the world have changed—but not necessarily diminished—the threats you face. Today, one of the most prevalent threat's you face is electronic crime.

A criminal electronic attack against you or your family can take place at any time due to the increased use of unprotected devices such as cell phones, p.d.a.'s, and personal computers by which we make ourselves vulnerable to electronic crime, as can a fire or other disaster.

However, you can influence what happens to you by assuming more responsibility for your own personal security while using these devices.

A) Protecting what is yours

Sure it sounds easy," just protect what is yours." The fact is that most people do not know what they have on hand or better yet are not aware of what a criminal might use to gain further access to what they are really after, your identity, your assets, and worse then that your future integrity.

"Since mobile devices are subject to all sorts of threats including both technological [viruses, worms, spam] and physical [lost or stolen], it is essential that you allow the use of these instruments devise precautionary policies regarding their use and further document courses of action if exposed to these kind of threats," policies and procedures should include the following:

Utilize advanced encryption and security standards, including Wired Equivalent Privacy (WEP) to minimize the occurrence of WLAN-related vulnerabilities;

Password-protect all mobile devices;

Encrypt sensitive documents that are stored on the device;

Minimize access to sensitive internal information by using firewalls;

Back-up data regularly on all mobile devices; and

Implement antivirus software on all mobile devices.

B) Classifying Your Data

Data classification is a critical step on the path to effective information lifecycle management; it is not just a means to an end. Data classification is a fundamental process that drives value by enabling the alignment of information to best address personal needs while aligning the cost of storage realalistically.

Initially, the process of data classification was used to help people better address business continuity and disaster recovery. With volumes of information being created, individuals wanted to be sure the right set and copy of data could be retrieved if a disaster occurred. This was accomplished through performance of full and incremental backups.

The idea of developing data policies is not new. Its roots can be traced back to the mainframe objectives of years ago. Back then, hierarchical storage management (HSM) was the precursor to what we call information lifecycle management today. Nowadays, the rudimentary data policies that supported HSM have given way to a broader expression of data classification that must take into consideration today's complex environments where our personal information traverses the internet and the airwaves alarmingly free and available for the use of any one whom it falls victim. With the variety of blue tooth devices being used it is just a hackers (perpetrators) play ground while this data travels within easy access.

Nuts and bolts of data classification

Data classification is designed to give individuals a full understanding of the value of data for seamless operations. To be successful, three key factors must be addressed: value, time, and cost.

Data classification aligns data value according to drivers such as performance and availability, regulatory compliance, information protection, budgets, and new what is the value of the gain for the individual who steals the data and what is the potential loss or risk involved for the data owner individually. It achieves this via the following approach:

- Providing a clear picture of the categories that exist.

- Describing the linkages between you personal and financial functions and their associated data.

- Demonstrating the economic value of data to an individual.

- Enabling shared technology architecture for each category of data.

- Defining a suite of storage-related services (e.g., availability, recoverability, manageability, scalability, and chargeability) for each category of data.

A time continuum, the period from data creation to disposal, and the varying degrees of value associated with the data at each stage in its life-cycle, also must be considered. Last but not least, data classification involves the mapping of data to a logical and physical architecture. Cost comes into consideration in relation to the architecture chosen to support the data.

Two key exercises, are fundamental to personal data classification. The first, is the process by which individuals identify or understand how they meet specific personal requirements, and then determine if they are on the right storage platform.

Classifying your data is all about asking yourself the right questions such as: How often does the information need to be accessed? How much is budgeted to protect this data? Where is the data available currently? What are the risks involved if this information is stolen?

Using formalized qualification criteria for each piece or section of the data is the best way to narrow this down and limit your risk.

For example all the data you have and use on a regular basis should be categorized as either public information: meaning anyone can see and no harm can be done by it, private information :data if added to other data may cause some loss financially or otherwise, and of course confidential: data that if stolen will cause pain financially or otherwise cause a loss.

Individuals face key challenges in managing information due to the relentless growth of data, the increasing threat of of information being stolen due to its increasing availability the wrong people and or its under protected. Data classification helps people to directly address these challenges by aligning data to appropriate storage tiers and defining rules and policies for optimum data and resource management and securing it with the proper controls for less exposure to theft.

A key enabler for furthering personal initiatives, data classification also brings individual a step closer to protecting their data and knowing what to protect.

4) C.I.A

While managing your data there are three key factors to bear in mind. These factors are what risks exists if the Confidentiality, loss of Integrity, and Availability of the data occurs.

Confidentiality refers to limiting information access and disclosure to the set of authorized users, and preventing access by or disclosure to unauthorized ones. Authentication methods that identify users, and access control mechanisms that limit each user's use, underpin the goal of confidentiality. (Confidentiality is related to the broader concept of privacy.)

Integrity refers to the trustworthiness of information resources. It includes the concept of "data integrity"—namely, that data have not been changed inappropriately, whether by accident or deliberately malign activity. It also includes "origin" or "source integrity"—that is, that the data actually came from the the person or entity you think it did, rather than an imposter.

Integrity can even include the notion that the person or entity in question entered the right information—that is, information that reflected the actual circumstances (in statistics, this is the concept of "validity") and that under the same circumstances would generate identical data (what statisticians call "reliability"). On a more restrictive view, however, integrity of an information system includes only preservation without corruption of whatever was transmitted or entered into the system, right or wrong.

Availability refers, unsurprisingly, to the availability of information resources. An information system that is not available when you need it is at least as bad as none at all. It may be much worse, depending on how reliant the organization has become on a functioning computer and communications infrastructure. An unreliable system makes users nostalgic for the days of paper records.

Availability, like other aspects of security, may be affected by purely technical issues (e.g., a malfunctioning part of a computer or communications device), natural phenomena (e.g., wind or water), or human causes (accidental or deliberate). While the relative risks associated with these categories depend on the particular context, the general rule is that humans are the weakest link.

Security efforts to assure confidentiality, integrity and availability can be divided into those oriented to prevention and those focused on detection. The latter aims to rapidly discover and correct for lapses that could not be—or at least were not—prevented.

While this entry summarizes the general concepts, it is critical to remember that "appropriate" or "adequate" levels of confidentiality, integrity and availability depend on the context. So too the appropriate balance between prevention and detection. The nature of the efforts, or the classification of the data that is supported; the natural, technical and human risks to those endeavors; governing legal, professional and customary standards—all of these will condition how CIA standards are set in a particular situation.

A security question that is (literally) closer to home may be helpful in this regard: Is your personal residence secure? In some situations, simple locks on the doors and closed windows would be enough for a "yes" answer. In others, supplemental deadbolt locks, high-strength windows, burglar alarms, a vicious dog and a personal weapon would be required for an affirmative response. What if the same question were asked about the bank where you keep your savings? We suspect your standard for security there would be different than for your home. Or in reality should it be if in fact the data on your computer leaves your bank account information available for whom ever gains unlawful access to your computer. Are better yet what if this individual gains access to your personal information stored on your cell phone or p.d.a. and uses it to pretend he/she is you and cleans out your bank account. So one can see the value of where you store this obviously confidential information and what security controls are in place to protect your data from being disclosed to the wrong individual.

So it is for information security and CIA: context is (almost) everything.

Identification, authentication, accountability

To ensure the protection and reliability of your data security controls must be put in place. Obliviously when you protect the entrance of your home or car a lock and key are used. In the case of your personal information storage device this is also true. The lock and key is known as your logon and password. The logon identifies whom the person is trying to access the data and the password points to a file that tells the system, device, what these users can do when they actually unlock the door. Along with identifying that the individual is who he or she actual says they are the logon is recorded for future reference so as to trace when the user entered the device and what they did.

WHAT: The definition of auditing for our purposes is the review and analysis of management, operational and technical controls, and the process an operating system uses to detect and record Security-related events. The records of such events are stored in a security log and are available only to those with the proper permissions. A computer system may have several audit trails, each devoted to a particular type of activity. The audit trail should allow the audit reviewers to reconstruct a complete sequence of security-related events.

WHY: Audit logs provide an independent review and examination of records and activities to assess the adequacy of the security features you have enacted and recommend necessary changes in controls, policies or procedures. Audit logs also provide a good way to determine if and how attacks take place and act as a key security and system administration tool for performance, which affects the "availability of service" security tenet. However, audit logs don't perform real-time intrusion detection and notification, of which we will cover in greater detail further on.

STRATEGY: Generally, you can audit logon events, object access, policy change, privilege use, process tracking, system events, system startup and shutdown and audit account management.

No matter what events you audit, the record should at least contain: records of each action, together with trace or identification parameters; connection start and end times; and association of network activities with corresponding user audit trails. The audit trail should be to retain an online audit trail for at least 24 hours, and it's a good practice to keep all offline audit trail data on magnetic media for at least one year (or longer as specified by your policy). It is recommending including the audit logs in your backups, to a tape device, so that you can retrieve the information later in the case of a breech of security. In other words if your credit card information is stolen there may possibly be a clue as to how the data was taken within these valued logs. Better yet is the scenario where while reviewing these logs you discover a way in which your valued personal information is exposed and you block it prior to the system being compromised. So you can see that the log information can play a large part in how you protect your system.

Privacy

Is the quality of being secluded from the presence or view of others is how Webster defines it. So basically we want to seclude or block from the view of others certain items as a rule. Again, not to repeat myself, but the data you will store on your device, whether it be a cell phone, laptop, pda, or electronic calendar must be categorized and controlled as such. I will explain in greater detail as we go on what security controls are a used to avoid particular vulnerabilities as we continue.

As a rule of thumb never keep your Social Security Number, bank account numbers, or credit card information on an electronic device that has access to the internet. Memorize the number, most due; I did when I was about 16. Committing these 9 numbers to memory may save you millions of dollars and once more save you from the risk of Identity theft. Identity theft is the top consumer fraud complaint in America and a stolen identity can take months or years to correct. Never answer a questionnaire from a creditor or payment method that you receive thru email lest you wriiten confirmation that it actually came from the source company it says it did. Thus method is called phishing. Phishing defined is (fish´ing) (n.) The act of sending an e-mail to a user falsely claiming to be an established legitimate enterprise in an attempt to scam the user into surrendering private information that will be used for identity theft. The e-mail directs the user to visit a Web site where they are asked to update personal information, such as passwords and credit card, social security, and bank account numbers, that the legitimate organization already has. The Web site, however, is bogus and set up only to steal the user's information.

1) Contact the fraud departments of any one of the three major credit bureaus to place a fraud alert on your credit file. The fraud alert requests creditors to contact you before opening any new accounts or making any changes to your existing accounts. As soon as the credit bureau confirms your fraud alert, the other two credit bureaus will be automatically notified to place fraud alerts, and all three credit reports will be sent to you free of charge.

2) Close the accounts that you know or believe have been tampered with or opened fraudulently. Use the ID Theft Affidavit when disputing new unauthorized accounts

3) File a police report. Get a copy of the report to submit to your creditors and others that may require proof of the crime.

4) File your complaint with the FTC. The FTC maintains a database of identity theft cases used by law enforcement agencies for investigations. Filing a complaint also helps us learn more about identity theft and the problems victims are having so that they can better assist you. To illustrate how much of an issue an nusance to society the crime of idenity theft is causing I wanted to share a brief story from a news paper clipping with you:

Even Babies Aren't Safe From Identity Theft
By Eyewitness News' Sade Baderinwa

(New York—WABC, April 15, 2005)—Identity thieves have a new target, victims so young they can't even read, write or walk yet. We're talking about infants' identities being stolen—days after they're born.

He was just 21-days old and Andrew Brook was all ready a crime victim. Someone had stolen his identity, gone to a clinic and received a prescription for a powerful narcotic. His father assumed the bill that arrived was a mistake.

John Brook, Father: "The first thing we did was call the clinic and say what's going on? They said it had been provided by the person who walked into the clinic."

Although his name appeared only on two documents—his birth certificate and medical records—Andrew's identity had been stolen and his father's astonishment turned to anger when the police seemed totally uninterested in investigating.

John Brook, Father: "It took two months to get them to actually file that police report. That was only after weekly phone calls from me just badgering them until they actually filed one."

Undoing identity theft is not easy. Michelle Bartleheimer's three year-old daughter was also a victim, and Michelle spent about a thousand hours contacting credit bureaus to set the record straight. Michelle Bartleheimer, Mother: "I cried tears every day, I was on the phone, the internet, researching it, trying to track it down." But even after the identity theft is remedied, the effects can be far reaching. John Brook, Father: "You don't relax anymore, you worry about who you're giving your information to, how its being used." The experience can offer an unwelcome reality check—that despite one's best efforts, a parent can't protect a child from everything. Michelle Bartleheimer, Mother: "I thought I was doing everything to protect her. I never thought I would have to protect her from identity theft." Identity theft in this country reportedly costs up to $53 billion.

2

Access Control

What is Access Control? These restrict access to system and devices objects based on user identity. Also they determine the authorization to certain files and usually create some form of an audit trail in log format so that access to these devices, files, systems can be traced back to the user identifier so you can tell who did what when.

The most common of these are the password which is an item that allows your access to the systems. Based on the access rights that go along with your user id the system will make a decision on what you can do or authorize you to perform certain functions once your in the system. Some of these are whether or not you can read, write, and or execute certain functions once in.

The current proliferation of "phishing" scams and "keystroke loggers" Trojan horse programs has had led to a huge growth in identity theft and been resulting in fraud losses from the compromise of bank accounts, credit cards, etc.. The Federal Trade Commission estimated that in 2003 there 10 million Identity theft victims in the U.S. alone at a cost of $50 billion. Anybody who has ever used e-mail had received letters that ask them to go to a site that appears real but is a fake. The fake site is used to harvest user names, passwords, social security numbers, and other personal information so that the owners can use to perpetrate their victims and take on their identity. For this reason it is for obvious reasons very important to keep your passwords to yourself and never share them with anyone. Use of a password vault is best never write it down for then it can get in the wrong hands http://www.cyber-ark.com/networksecurity/passwordvault_ggl2.asp#

The greatest cause of this current dismissal state of affairs regarding identity theft is often maligned passwords. The list below are just a few suggestions to make a password stronger and less likely to get broken by such a crook:

1.   Use a password of at least 6 characters

2.   Do not use your user name or any portion of.

3.   Do not use the names of family members.

4.   Do not use license plate numbers or phone numbers.

5.   Do not use consecutive numbers or letters of the alphabet(1234abcde)

6.   Do not use single numbers or letters consecutively(1111111aaaaaaa)

7.   Do not allow keyboard progression(qwerty)

8.   Do not use a password using a single word from an English or foreign dictionary.

9.   Do use an easy to remember password and don't write it down.

10. As a mnemonic device use numbers in a phrase.

11. Do choose difficult to guess passwords.

12. Do not choose passwords that relate to personal life or work.

13. Do not use password that are identical to other passwords you have used before.

All in all I think the message here "DO NOT LET ANYONE HAVE OR BE ABLE TO QUESS YOUR PASSWORD". Your password is the key to all the information within whatever electronic device it protects whether your ATM accounts pin or your cell phone and all the data within. One sure fire way to open yourself to fraud, theft, and any other deceptive crime you can think of that can be performed with access to the information once it is disclosed by a password is the major risk here. So let's make passwords as difficult as possible. There are even software packages that can be obtained to "crack" passwords based on the dictionary and common words that are freely available on the internet so be warned.

Here is some additional food for thought on the subject:

According to Gartner in the past twelve months...
57 Million U.S. Adults received a phising email
1.4 Million U.S. adults have suffered indentity fraud
$1.2 billion lost by U.S. banks caused by indentity fraud
And Forrester states that in the same period...
9% of US online consumers have experienced identity theft Winpop
42% of these victims would do more online if they believed they were secure 90% of Americans agree identity theft needs to be taken more seriously And in the case of Identity Fraud:
85% of cases are opened on a "reactive" problem-discovering basis whilst 15% of cases reflect "proactive" responses by businesses Data Protection Act

Authentication can be based on any of these three items:

A) Something you know

B) Something you have

C) Something you are

Strong authentication is when a system, device, or object of some type take 2 or more of these access items to allow access. This is known as two factor authentification. The most commonly used example of this is the ATM card.It consists of something you have(the card) and something you know(the pin). To even further this you could incorporate something you are such as your fingerprint or retina. In any case both factors are neeed to allow any access to the system/object.

Monitor your accounts periodically One of the benefits of having access to all of our accounts online is that you don't have to wait for a paper bill to arrive to find out about possible identity theft. Keep an eye on your online statements to look for charges or withdrawals you didn't authorize. The earlier you catch a problem, the easier it often is to fix.

Check Your Computer for Spy ware
Keyboard loggers, screen captures, and Trojan horses are all spyware infections that can be used by hackers to lift personal data from your computer like your password, which in turn leads to the disclosure of all your personal information. Scan regularly with anti-spy ware software and make sure you use a personal firewall to keep unwanted visitors off your computer.

3

Information Privacy Principles under the Privacy Act 1988

Generally, the federal Privacy Act covers the collection, use and disclosure, quality and security of personal information. The federal Privacy Act also gives you rights to access and correct personal information about you. You also have the right to make a complaint if you think your personal information has been mishandled.

The eleven Information Privacy Principles in the federal Privacy Act protect your personal information and give you rights in the way Commonwealth and ACT government agencies handle your information. Your Privacy & Government gives you more information.

Principle 1—Manner and purpose of collection of personal information

1. Personal information shall not be collected by a collector for inclusion in a record or in a generally available publication unless:

(a) the information is collected for a purpose that is a lawful purpose directly related to a function or activity of the collector; and

(b) the collection of the information is necessary for or directly related to that purpose.

2. Personal information shall not be collected by a collector by unlawful or unfair means.

Principle 2—Solicitation of personal information from individual concerned

Where:

(a) a collector collects personal information for inclusion in a record or in a generally available publication; and

(b) the information is solicited by the collector from the individual concerned;

the collector shall take such steps (if any) as are, in the circumstances, reasonable to ensure that, before the information is collected or, if that is not practicable, as soon as practicable after the information is collected, the individual concerned is generally aware of:

(c) the purpose for which the information is being collected;

(d) if the collection of the information is authorized or required by or under law—the fact that the collection of the information is so authorized or required; and

(e) any person to whom, or any body or agency to which, it is the collector's usual practice to disclose personal information of the kind so collected, and (if known by the collector) any person to whom, or any body or agency to which, it is the usual practice of that first mentioned person, body or agency to pass on that information.

Principle 3—Solicitation of personal information generally

Where:

(a) a collector collects personal information for inclusion in a record or in a generally available publication; and

(b) the information is solicited by the collector:

the collector shall take such steps (if any) as are, in the circumstances, reasonable to ensure that, having regard to the purpose for which the information is collected:

(c) the information collected is relevant to that purpose and is up to date and complete; and

(d) the collection of the information does not intrude to an unreasonable extent upon the personal affairs of the individual concerned.

Principle 4—Storage and security of personal information

A record-keeper who has possession or control of a record that contains personal information shall ensure:

(a) that the record is protected, by such security safeguards as it is reasonable in the circumstances to take, against loss, against unauthorised access, use, modification or disclosure, and against other misuse; and

(b) that if it is necessary for the record to be given to a person in connection with the provision of a service to the record-keeper, everything reasonably within the power of the record-keeper is done to prevent unauthorised use or disclosure of information contained in the record.

Principle 5—Information relating to records kept by record-keeper

1. A record-keeper who has possession or control of records that contain personal information shall, subject to clause 2 of this Principle, take such steps as are, in the circumstances, reasonable to enable any person to ascertain:

(a) whether the record-keeper has possession or control of any records that contain personal information; and

(b) if the record-keeper has possession or control of a record that contains such information:

(i) the nature of that information;

(ii) the main purposes for which that information is used; and

(iii) the steps that the person should take if the person wishes to obtain access to the record.

2. A record-keeper is not required under clause 1 of this Principle to give a person information if the record-keeper is required or authorised to refuse to give that information to the person under the applicable provisions of any law of the Commonwealth that provides for access by persons to documents.

3. A record-keeper shall maintain a record setting out:

(a) the nature of the records of personal information kept by or on behalf of the record-keeper;

(b) the purpose for which each type of record is kept;

(c) the classes of individuals about whom records are kept;

(d) the period for which each type of record is kept;

(e) the persons who are entitled to have access to personal information contained in the records and the conditions under which they are entitled to have that access; and

(f) the steps that should be taken by persons wishing to obtain access to that information.

4. A record-keeper shall:

(a) make the record maintained under clause 3 of this Principle available for inspection by members of the public; and

(b) give the Commissioner, in the month of June in each year, a copy of the record so maintained.

Principle 6—Access to records containing personal information

Where a record-keeper has possession or control of a record that contains personal information, the individual concerned shall be entitled to have access to that record, except to the extent that the record-keeper is required or authorised to refuse to provide the individual with access to that record under the applicable provisions of any law of the Commonwealth that provides for access by persons to documents.

Principle 7—Alteration of records containing personal information

1. A record-keeper who has possession or control of a record that contains personal information shall take such steps (if any), by way of making appropriate corrections, deletions and additions as are, in the circumstances, reasonable to ensure that the record:

(a) is accurate; and

(b) is, having regard to the purpose for which the information was collected or is to be used and to any purpose that is directly related to that purpose, relevant, up to date, complete and not misleading.

2. The obligation imposed on a record-keeper by clause 1 is subject to any applicable limitation in a law of the Commonwealth that provides a right to require the correction or amendment of documents.

3. Where:

(a) the record-keeper of a record containing personal information is not willing to amend that record, by making a correction, deletion or addition, in accordance with a request by the individual concerned; and

(b) no decision or recommendation to the effect that the record should be amended wholly or partly in accordance with that request has been made under the applicable provisions of a law of the Commonwealth;

the record-keeper shall, if so requested by the individual concerned, take such steps (if any) as are reasonable in the circumstances to attach to the record any statement provided by that individual of the correction, deletion or addition sought.

Principle 8—Record-keeper to check accuracy etc of personal information before use

A record-keeper who has possession or control of a record that contains personal information shall not use that information without taking such steps (if any) as are, in the circumstances, reasonable to ensure that, having regard to the purpose for which the information is proposed to be used, the information is accurate, up to date and complete.

Principle 9—Personal information to be used only for relevant purposes

A record-keeper who has possession or control of a record that contains personal information shall not use the information except for a purpose to which the information is relevant.

Principle 10—Limits on use of personal information

1. A record-keeper who has possession or control of a record that contains personal information that was obtained for a particular purpose shall not use the information for any other purpose unless:

(a) the individual concerned has consented to use of the information for that other purpose;

(b) the record-keeper believes on reasonable grounds that use of the information for that other purpose is necessary to prevent or lessen a serious and imminent threat to the life or health of the individual concerned or another person;

(c) use of the information for that other purpose is required or authorised by or under law;

(d) use of the information for that other purpose is reasonably necessary for enforcement of the criminal law or of a law imposing a pecuniary penalty, or for the protection of the public revenue; or

(e) the purpose for which the information is used is directly related to the purpose for which the information was obtained.

2. Where personal information is used for enforcement of the criminal law or of a law imposing a pecuniary penalty, or for the protection of the public revenue, the record-keeper shall include in the record containing that information a note of that use.

Principle 11—Limits on disclosure of personal information

1. A record-keeper who has possession or control of a record that contains personal information shall not disclose the information to a person, body or agency (other than the individual concerned) unless:

(a) the individual concerned is reasonably likely to have been aware, or made aware under Principle 2, that information of that kind is usually passed to that person, body or agency;

(b) the individual concerned has consented to the disclosure;

(c) the record-keeper believes on reasonable grounds that the disclosure is necessary to prevent or lessen a serious and imminent threat to the life or health of the individual concerned or of another person;

(d) the disclosure is required or authorised by or under law; or

(e) the disclosure is reasonably necessary for the enforcement of the criminal law or of a law imposing a pecuniary penalty, or for the protection of the public revenue.

2. Where personal information is disclosed for the purposes of enforcement of the criminal law or of a law imposing a pecuniary penalty, or for the purpose of the protection of the public revenue, the record-keeper shall include in the record containing that information a note of the disclosure.

3. A person, body or agency to whom personal information is disclosed under clause 1 of this Principle shall not use or disclose the information for a purpose other than the purpose for which the information was given to the person, body or agency.

With Identity theft being a major threat and vulnerability the increase in its popularity has made the Internet a dangerous place to work and play in the new millennium.

We can all help to eliminate Identity Theft by controlling the use of our social security numbers in our communities today.

Here are some suggested ways that our SSN's being controlled can limit or even prevent ID theft:

1) Don't ask for your customers SSN's and don't use employee social security numbers as their time card numbers.
2) Develop a crisis management plan to be used if sensitive data on employees or customers is lost or stolen.
3) Pressure service providers including fund managers to stop using employee's SSN's as identifiers.
4) Employ a clean desk policy, require a password and screen savers.
5) Conduct background check on employees and new hires.
6) Store sensitive data in secure computer system and encrypt data.

7) Store physical documents in secure spaces such as locked file cabinets.

8) Dispose of or destroy documents and or media that contain sensitive data properly.

9) Conduct regular Security Awareness training for new hires, staff and contractors.

10) As mentioned earlier classify data and encrypt when needed.

Privacy threats on the web

When you are surfing the web you may think you are anonymous, but there are various ways that information about you or your activities can be collected without your knowledge or consent:

• **Cookies**

A cookie is a piece of information that an Internet website sends to your browser when you access information at that site. Upon receipt of the information your browser saves the information on your hard-disk (unless your browser doesn't support cookies). Each time you use your computer to access that same website, the information that was previously received is sent back to the website by your browser. Most commonly used browsers support the use of cookies.

Why are cookies used? Generally, for those of us that access the Internet through a public ISP, each request we make to a website cannot be linked to a previous request, as each request does not contain a permanent unique identifier. Cookies allow website operators to assign a unique permanent identifier to a computer which can be used to associate the requests made to the website from that computer.

Cookies indicate to a website that you have been there before and can be used to record what parts of a website you visit. While cookies in themselves may not identify you, in the way a name or address does, a cookie could potentially be linked with other identifying information.

For example, if you provide extra information about yourself to the website by buying something on-line or subscribing to a free service, then the cookies can be used to build up a profile of your buying habits and what you are interested in. They can then be used to tailor banner advertising to your interests.

Many web surfers object strongly to cookies as they feel that they invade their hard drive without their permission. There are various things you can do to combat cookies if you distrust them, these include:

- Setting the browser cookie file to be Read Only. Whether you can do this or not may depend on what sort of Operating System (OS) or browser you are using. But if you can do this then the cookies will only last for as long as your browser is running.

- Set up your computer to delete the cookies file whenever you start your browser.

- Many browsers allow you to set them up so that you are notified when a cookie is to be written to your computer. However there may be instances where there are so many cookies that it becomes annoying to reject them all.

- There are many software products you can get which will reject or manage cookies for you, these include Cookie Crusher, Cookie Pal, and Cookie Cruncher

• HTTP

When you access a web page from a website, the website expects you to provide certain information so that it can provide the page you request. The HyperText transfer protocol (HTTP) is the set of rules that websites and browsers follow in order to communicate. One obvious piece of information the website will require is what page you want to look at. The technical term for the location of this page is the Uniform Resource Locator (URL). http://www.privacy.gov.au is the URL for the Federal Privacy Commissioner's home page.

There are various aspects of HTTP which may allow your surfing activities to be tracked. Other information which may be sent whenever you request a web page includes your e-mail address and the last web page you looked at. Whether this information is transmitted is dependant on whether your browser supports these options and whether you have got your browser configured with your e-mail address. You can visit http://www.uiuc.edu/cgi-bin/info to check out what information your browser is sending with each web page request.

• Browsers

The most widely used browsers are the various versions of Netscape Navigator and Communicator and Microsoft Internet Explorer. Other less widely used browsers include Mosaic, which was one of the original browsers and Lynx which is a text based browser. There have been many reports of security bugs in browsers which can allow hackers and websites to access your personal information while you are surfing the web. Netscape and Microsoft often provide fixes for these bugs soon after they become aware of them, these can be downloaded from their websites. It's difficult to assess the risk to your personal information of using any particular browser, but it may be wise to keep up to date with news about security bugs. Microsoft windows is very openly vulnerable to attack,Two precautionary ways to battle this is to stay current on the software patches. This web site provides a tool for updating patcheshttp://www.stbernard.com/products/updateexpert/products_updateexpert.asp

The other thing you can do is harden the operating system. The NSA web page has win instructions on how for the different OS's. use the search feature for your needs at www.nsa.org

DISASTER RECOVERY-We need to all be prepared for the shocking loss of data. Most cases this is a devastation so like in life 'we need insurance. BE sure to keep your data backed-up,

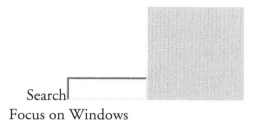

Search

Focus on Windows

Backup Utility for WinXP Home

Part 3: Installing the Utility for XP Home Edition

If you have Microsoft Windows XP *Professional* Edition, you will easily be able to find the Backup Utility by clicking Start -> All Programs -> Accessories -> System Tools -> Backup. However, if you are using Windows XP *Home* Edition, your search for a backup utility under System Tools will be fruitless. Although Microsoft originally planned to include the Backup Utility in the Home Edition as well as the Professional Edition, they removed it, for reasons known to themselves, from the final version that you can buy today.

development for many, fear not! You, as a reader of the About.com Focus on Windows site, are one of The Elite, The Astute, and you will be shown the secret necessary to be able to install and use the same Backup Utility that is available to XP Professional users. Hidden deep in the recesses of the Windows XP Home Edition CD lies the actual installation program that you need to put the Backup Utility on your computer. Simply insert the XP CD, and run NTBACKUP.MSI (it might look like just "Ntbackup") program from the folder D:\Valueadd\msft\ntbackup where D: is the letter of your CD drive. This will launch the Windows Backup Utility Installation Wizard, which will install the utility automatically. When it is finished, click "Finish." It's that easy!

Now you can click Start -> All Programs -> Accessories -> System Tools -> Backup, and the Backup Utility will start. One of the things that you may note is the presence of the Automated System Recovery Wizard which was mentioned in <u>Part 1 of this feature</u>. While you can try to use this Wizard with the Home Edition of XP, the results can be unpredictable, and the disks created with this Wizard in XP Home are unreliable. Microsoft notes and acknowledges this

• There may already be information about you published on the web

Governments, schools, businesses and other organizations may have already collected personal information about you. Information collected by governments is sometimes publicly available in the form of Public Registers. The Electoral Roll, and the Telephone Directory are Public Registers. Your school, university or employer may publish your name or other information about you. Much personal information which is publicly available has been collected and combined into databases by web based companies which then sell this information to businesses or individuals. Comprehensive and sometimes inaccurate profiles of individuals can be derived by combining information from many sources.

As there is little or no law anywhere in the world governing this sort of activity there's not much you can do about it, but at least you can be aware of it.

• Downloading freeware or shareware

There is a lot of free and cheap software available for download on the Internet. It may be difficult to avoid using freeware and shareware as much of this software underpins the Internet (some popular web server applications are free as are the two most popular browsers, Netscape Navigator and Microsoft Explorer). However, it may be prudent to keep track of information about freeware and shareware and only use the software that is widely used and has a good reputation

• Search engines

These are web-based software tools that allow you to search for information on the Internet. Some of the most well known ones are Google, Yahoo, Alta Vista, Hotbot, Excite, Infoseek and Web-Crawler. Many of these offer facilities to search for people. If your name appears somewhere on the Internet then these search engines can find it. Your name may be associated with other information about you so it may be possible for anyone using search engines to find out quite a bit about you. Some search engines also allow the searching of news groups for postings associated with an e-mail address.

• Electronic commerce

If you buy something from a commercial web site you will probably have to use a credit card. This means you will be transmitting your credit card number over the Internet. Many people are doing this but a lot of others don't think it's safe.

Currently a widely used security system is Secure Socket Layer (SSL) which is built into the major browsers. In Australia most web browsers use 40 bit encryption. While SSL may provide protection during the transmission of Credit Card numbers there are also concerns about the secure storage of Credit Card numbers. There have been instances where hackers have stolen lists of Credit Card numbers from ISPs and commercial web sites.

Governments and businesses are keen to encourage Electronic Commerce but there is some resistance by consumers due to concerns about security and privacy. Currently Internet businesses seem to require you to provide more personal information than you would for over the counter purchases. Many people are concerned that this information will then be re-used for another purpose or sold to direct marketers.

• E-mail

How you set up your e-mail address may affect your privacy. Like street addresses e-mail addresses are essentially locators, but they locate you in cyberspace rather than real space. The format of an e-mail address is A@B.C.D, where A is your name or handle, B is usually your Internet Service Provider (ISP) or the organization you work for, C and D are called domains. The C domain may refer to your area of work or activity. For example if you worked for the Government then this would probably be .gov. Many commercial ISPs use either .com or .net. D is the country domain, for Australia this is .au. So an e-mail address for someone who works for the Office of the Privacy Commissioner might be FredNirks@privacy.gov.au. If Fred had a private e-mail account with the ISP Ozemail his private e-mail address might be fnirks@ozemail.com.au. If Fred wanted a more private e-mail address he may use a handle or nym (from pseudonym) such as zorro@ozemail.com.au.

The advantage of using a nym is that you can then only reveal your identity to who you want to know it. If you go to the trouble of using a nym you should be careful to set up your e-mail application (this may be part of your browser or a stand alone e-mail application like Eudora) so that the name and identity fields are left blank. Otherwise this information may be included in your e-mail.

If you want to use a nym it is important to use an ISP that has disabled the Finger utility. If this is not disabled then anyone may be able to use your e-mail address to find out your name and other information about you.

• E-mail and cryptography

E-mail is more like a post card than a letter in an envelope. Anyone who intercepts your e-mail can read it if it's sent as plain text. This may not matter to you but if you would prefer your e-mail to be readable only by those you send it to then you might consider encrypting it. PGP (Pretty Good Privacy) is a popular and free program that uses cryptographic techniques to protect information. The way it works is a bit complicated. If you want to know more about how PGP works then read one of our other documents titled Cryptography and Pretty Good Privacy (Download in Word or PDF).

Cryptographic techniques also offer mechanisms for emulating signatures on electronic documents. Digital signatures, as they are known, are generally based on public key cryptographic methods. In 1996 Standards Australia released a document titled Strategies for the implementation of a Public Key Authentication Framework (PKAF) in Australia. Late in 1997 the Minister for Communications, the Information Economy and the Arts announced that the Government has agreed to facilitate the creation of a new peak body, which will oversee the development of a national system for on-line authentication. It is likely that the support structures for these initiatives will require the collection of personal identifying information.

• Spam

Spam is junk e-mail. Many people who have purchased something over the Internet or have their e-mail address published on a website or have subscribed to a news service or who have participated in news groups or mailing lists, get spam. This is because these public sources can be harvested for e-mail addresses. Some ISPs and other Internet businesses have sold lists of their customer's e-mail addresses to spammers. This is now considered to be very bad form. Spammers have been known to use programs to randomly generate e-mail addresses.

Spam has become so prevalent that it can compromise and slow down the whole network. There is now a big anti-spam movement and there are various spam filters you can get to filter out and delete spam. Unfortunately, spam persists. It's an unfortunate fact that if you participate in discussion groups or subscribe to news services then you will probably get spam. The fact that spam is a use of your e-mail address for a purpose that you don't agree to and that you are actually paying for the delivery of the spam makes it particularly annoying.

Spam is now illegal in Australia. New Australian legislation relating to spam—the Spam Act, 2003—came into effect on 10 April 2004. It is now illegal to send, or cause to be sent, 'unsolicited commercial electronic messages'. The Spam Act is enforced by the Australian Communications Authority (ACA). To report spam, or for information on the Spam Act, spam reduction, and internet security tips visit www.spam.aca.gov.au

• *Dangers of Internet Relay Chat*

Chat groups have become very popular. As they operate in real-time they are similar to telephone party lines. Many people who participate in chat groups use nyms or handles, so you don't really know who you are chatting with or even their gender. Some people have established relationships on chat groups which they have continued in real life. However, it is important to note that your personal safety may be at risk, if you meet people from chat rooms, otherwise unknown to you.

4

Telecommunications and Network Security

As individuals there are many ways in which we access the internet. Some examples of this are via high speed cable access, DSL (Data Subscriber Line), and or through a dial up modem.

No mater how you access the internet there are obvious precautions and safeguards we must all take in order to protect ourselves from the possibility of having our personal data stolen or just vandalized. We can implement firewalls, intrusion detection systems, anti-virus software, spy-ware software, in addition to hardening our operating system and keeping up on security patches for the applications we run and the operating system.

What is a firewall and what do I look for when shopping for a personal firewall?

Well like most good internet surf heads I referred to Askjeeves for the answer of what is a firewall, for the down and dirty definition and here are the results:

noun: (computing) a security system consisting of a combination of hardware and software that limits the exposure of a computer or computer network to attack from crackers

noun: fireproof (or fire-resistant) wall designed to prevent the spread of fire through a building or a vehicle

Well as one can see it is apparent where the internet springing up in our day to day life has taken one definition and spawned the need for another. True that a firewall still prevents spread of something harmful like fire only in this case the use of one is necessary to stop the spread or limit the spread of an attack from an outside intruder of anther kind. Now I say limit because remember this protection device is only as good as the individual whom performed the configuration or set it up. There are many types of firewalls, as listed below, and multiple vendors of such, but we are mostly concerned with the Firewalls that an individual in the home needs (personal firewall) in order to protect what is theirs and what they need to know to set one up. At this point you can skip down to the Personal Firewall Setup section but please at least glance at the different types until you begin to fell sleepy.

Firewall Types

Packet Filtering Firewalls or Screening Routers

- First Generation Firewall

- Works at the Network or Transport Layer

- Uses Access Control Lists (ACLs) that tell the firewall which packets can and cannot be forwarded to certain addresses

  - Ex.: allow <source ip/mask> <destination ip/mask> Protocol Port....

- Looks at the data packet to get the information about the source and destination addresses, the sessions communications protocol (TCP,UDP, ICMP) and the source and destination application port

Application Level Firewalls or Proxy Server

- Second Generation Firewall

- Application Layer Gateway

- Works at the Application Layer.

- Transfers a copy of each data packet from one network to another, masking the data's origin. This protects the network from outsiders who may be trying to get information about the network's design.

- Reduces network perfomance since it analyzes every packet

- Variation: Circuit Level Firewall: Creates a virtual circuit between the workstation client and the server, provides security for a wide variety of protocols and is easier to maintain.

- IBM uses Proxy servers to get out to the Internet.

Stateful Inspection Firewalls

- Third Generation Firewall.

- Captures the data packets at the Network Layer, then uses all OSI layers to analyze.

- Offers a more complete inspection of the data.

- Examines "state" and "context" of the data packets and helps to track protocols that are considered "connection-less"

Dynamic Packet Filtering Firewalls

- Fourth Generation Firewall

- Enables the modification of the firewall security rule.

- Used for providing limited support for UDP. For a short period of time the firewall will remember all of the UDP packets that have crossed the network's perimeter, and it decides whether to enable packets to pass through the firewall

Kernel Proxy

- Fifth Generation Firewall

- Provides a modular, kernel-based, multi-layer session evaluation and runs in the Windows NT Executive.

Specialized, using dynamic and custom TCP/IP-based stacks to inspect the network packets and enforce security policies

You're here, this is where the meat about the firewall for is.

Personal Firewall Setup

The perfect personal firewall would be inexpensive, or even free, and so easy to install a 3rd grader could do it. Also it would hide all ports to make your PC stealthy to scans, which as everybody knows any 3rd grader also has a great public domain (free) scanner that check p.c.s on the network for what ports are open so as to launch an attack.

What are ports? Oh, when I talk of ports I am referring to TCP ports, Telecommunication Control Protocol. At this point it seem I have a little explaining before we continue. See there once was, is, something called the OSI, Open Systems Interconnect that tried to attempt to have a format that all computers would talk over, since in the earl days prior to Bill Gates taking over, there were many different types of computers and they all spoke different languages sort of speak. Then came the OSI so that everybody would uniformly talk the same jive (language) But everybody wanted to do their on thing and so a technology entitled TCP/IP was dreamt up and whola everybody, worldwide, could speak to each other.

In short what I am trying to say is that a firewall protects yourself from letting every Tom, Dick, and, Harry from getting on your computer by guarding these "ports".

Important Tips—Before installing personal firewall software on a Windows XP computer, be sure that the firewall built into Windows XP is turned off. Never use two software firewalls at the same time. Completely uninstall one before installing another. Use the vendor's uninstall utility or if not available, use the Windows XP add/remove software tool in the control panel. After you install a firewall, be sure to check it with a service like the Security Space Desktop Audit to make sure that it is configured correctly. Testing your firewall is the only sure way to tell that your computer is really being protected.

Another item that is good to have is an intrusion detection system. This is a software appliance that monitors what data comes in and goes out of your system and alerts when things look a bit suspicious. Black Ice PC protector is on such component that is easily loadable and very user friendly. It basically gives you both of these packages in one (Firewall and IDS). Black ICE PC Protection scans all inbound Internet traffic for suspicious activity on home or small business systems. The only issue with this component is what they call false positives. What is meant by this in layman's terms is that you will receive an indication of intrusion on everything, to include your ISP (Internet Service Provider) sending an ICMP(ping) to see if your machine is out there. This can be alarming but once you realize what real and what's not an attempt to hack your PC an IDS can be a life saver. Black ICE PC protection

- BLOCKS hacker attacks instantly

- PREVENTS destructive applications like worms and Trojans from ever starting

- REPORTS attempted attacks and identifies intruders

- SECURES any Internet connection, including dial-up, DSL, or cable modem

Modes of Connecting to the Internet

There are multiple methods of establishing a connection with your ISP in today's world. There is the drudgery of the old fashion dial up connection which gives you anywhere from 9.6 baud to 56 k.

The 56 k one is usable but much slower and responsive then the more commonly used cable modem and or Data Subscriber Line.

These forms run 100 mb(mega baud) or more and are the most common ways in most Metropolitan areas of today. The cable modem is a shared line so obviously is more susceptible to mischievous hacker types. In most cases any one whom has cable can get in line and capture their neighbor's data as it runs by in a broadcast mode. DSL on the other hand is point to point and is less likely to be sniffed or looked at by the criminal element.

Another commonality is that individuals like to set up their own home wireless network, which when no encryption is used can illuminate itself to view by anyone that wants to drive up with a wireless laptop and see what signals are in the area. So you can see that in all cases, no matter how you connect, you need to be wary of the possibilities of your data being viewed by anyone who knows the technology and how to manipulate it for their profit.

It is imperative that we all do a little research on Virus control, firewalls, IDS, encryption, and other means of protecting our valuable data while we connect to this jungle we call the Internet no matter what means of technology we use to get out there. This is apparently true even in the world of wireless phone communication now as illustrated in the following artickle which I found:

Bepy sure to purchase a pop up blocker an spyware programs. Most websites plant this kind of garbage on your system upon visit For maketing purposes. There are new virus,s developed daily by internet vandals here is an exqmple

Symatec an mcafee have good virus control products. lavasoft is good for cleaning adware. http://us.mcafee.com/root/landingpages/ affLandPage.asp?affid=101&lpname=linkshare_mie&cid=5614&siteI D=M241PF1pr2o-sqQoBRlVJqjm4KYSUsCK6A

http://www.symantec.com/index.htm

tp://www.noadware.net/?hop=truval3

MNY INTERNET PEOVIDERS provide these services as a standard just call and ask them.

ENCRYPTION

makes the message of your data unreadable by those you don't want to. Like the old decoder rings we use to get in cerial boxes. A great example you can use for e-mail PGP http://www.pgp.com/

They have gateway mail encryption',desktop, and disk encryption products .this keeps prying eyes away from private data and is highly recommended. You never no who can view your data since the internet is a dangerous place to play. You can enrypt your data on a PDA OR SMARTPHONE also see http://softguide.com/prog_j watch/ pj_1028.htm

<u>MICROSOFT THE CHINA EGG</u>

Microsoft has made many security flaws along a with money and is notorious to hackers for it's number of vulnerabilities. Although the operating system is full of holes it is the most common one of

choice. First step of protection is to stay up on the patches released

http://update.microsoft.com/windowsupdate/v6/default.aspx?ln=en-us this site checks the level of patching updates on your p.c to verify you are current or not, good site re: latest patches available is: http://www.windowsecurity.com/Also contains many more security hints.

There are some precautions you can take in addition to keeping up on the patching levels such as the recommendations published by the National Security Agency http://www.nsa.gov/ found on there web site. Perform a procedure called hardening http://www.nsa.gov/snac/OS/winxp/Wwinxp.pdf for windows xp others are listed. Just utilize the sites search feature for your particular need.

pchapter 7 **disaster recovery** you want to protect your data from being lost. Be sure to back all the data you want to save up periodically. You will need a dat tape or more commonly cd writer/reader and a good bak-up utility .her is a site for backing up windows XP http://www.microsoft.com/windowsxp/using/setup/learnmore/bott_03july14.mspx.lo be sure your power does not fluctuate. A separate isolated circuit with its own 3rd wire ground is recommende to reduce noise, be sure not plug other items in this circuit that contain a motor or heating element this will cause electronic noise and can damage the computer. Another recommended item is a surge protection device. If the local electric company has a brown out and surges power you will be protected, An uninterrupted power supply is another device you can use to eliminate this issue.the best configuration is to have your p.c. s and communications device plugged into clean uninterptable power such as recommended above.

Chapter 8 physical security

Be sure you system is in locked area and or has a locking device

A cable lock can be picked up at most computer supply stores or office supply. Also password protection is important to keep prying eyes out. Most systems you can password protect the hard.

drive and should and also password protect system access.

Never write your password down memorize it. It should be 8 characters long with the last being a number. Make the password random characters so that you will not fall victim to a dictionary attack. this is a common attack used by hackers using a program to quess your password.

Chapter 9 glossary of terms

Authentication—generally the process of verifying who Is at the other end of a transmission. To verify the identity of a user device or other in a computer system.

Availability of data-the state in which data in the place needed by the user.

ACL-access control list—slist of users,programs, and or processes and the specifications of access categories to which is assigned a list denoting which users have what privileges to particular resources

Accountability the property that enables activities on a system to be traced to individuals who might then be responsible for their actions

Adutin Trail a chronological record of security controls on a system. A system log thast hows sequence of events and uid that performed event.

Application layer gateway a network component that prides connectivety at the 7th layer of the osi open-systems configursble to filter what wants and not interconnect To connect reciprocally: *tried to interconnect the two theories.*

AdwareOften, the software tracks your web surfing habits, reports them to a central ad tracking database, and uses that information to know which ads to send you based on what it thinks your interests are. This kind of software is most frequently found in free internet downloads. In fact, some of the first popular programs to make widespread use of adware techniques were the p2p file sharing clients that popularized MP3 music swapping online.also known as spy-ware.

Asynchronous—type of communication oriented data synchronization with no defined relationship between transmission of data frames.see synchronous

Business continuity plan designed to minimize the damage done by an event and the facilitates the rapid recovery of full operational capability.

Baud rate of signal change the rate at which data is transmitted

Blue tooth A global initiative by Ericsson, IBM, Intel, Nokia and Toshiba to set a standard for cable-free connectivity between mobile phones, mobile PCs, handheld computers and other peripherals. It will use short-range radio links in the 2.gGHZ Instrumentation Scientific and Medical (ISM) "free band".

Browser The software used to access the web, such as Internet Explorer or Netscape

Cable modem is a modem that uses part of the capacity of the local cable system to transmit data rather than TV channels to the home. It works much like a Local Area Network. Unlike the typical cable system where TV signals can only be broadcast to the home, a cable modem allows information to be transmitted in both directions.

CISSP

CISSP stands for Certified Information Systems Security Professional, which is a vendor-neutral certification governed by the International Information Systems Security Certification Consortium (ISC2). It is considered one of the premiere security certifications.
en.wikipedia.org/wiki/CISSP—
(ISC)2

Confidentiality Pertains to the treatment of information that an individual has disclosed in a relationship of trust and with the expectation that it will not be divulged to others in ways that are inconsistent with the understanding of the original disclosure without permission.

CookiesInternet Browser)—Holds information on the times and dates you have visited web sites. Other information can also be saved to your hard disk in these text files, including information about online purchases, validation information about you for members-only web sites, and more.

Data classification he process of cutting portfolio data unto into related and often mutually exclusive groups. For example all accounts in the portfolio initiated during the spring loan campaign could be grouped together into a classification "Spring-2000". Typically, members of the class exhibit homogenous properties. Such classifications help in comparing performance of one class over the other Data policies

Dsl DSL (Digital Subscriber Line) is a technology for bringing high-bandwidth information to homes and small businesses over ordinary copper telephone lines.

Disaster recovery disaster recovery plan (DRP)—sometimes referred to as a business continuity plan (BCP) or business process contingency plan (BPCP)—describes how an…

Electronic threat—see vulnersbility.

Encryption Any procedure used in cryptography to convert plaintext into ciphertext in order to prevent anyone except the intended recipient from reading that data. There are many types of data encryption, and they are the basis of network security. Common types include Data Encryption Standard and public-key encryption.

FTC Federal Trade Commission. The federal agency primarily responsible for regulating national advertis

FirewallGateway that limits access between networks in accordance with local security policy. [NS4009]

HTTPHyper Text Transfer Protocol (HTTP), the actual communications protocol that enables Web browsing.

Hardening configure operating system to protect from known **vulner-abilities**

Historical storage management Integrity

ISPInternet Service Provider. A company that provides an Internet connection

IDS intrusion detection or prevention

ICMP ICMP is an extension to the Internet Protocol. It allows for the generation of error messages, test packets and informational messages related to IP.

Identificationthe act of designating or identifying something Identity theft Identity theft occurs when somebody steals your name and other personal information for fraudulent purposes. Identity theft is a form of identity crime (where somebody uses a false identity to commit a crime).

Proxy Share one internet connection with ALL the computers on your local network

Stateful inspection Also referred to as dynamic packet filtering. Stateful inspection is a firewall architecture that works at the network layer. Unlike static packet filtering, which examines a

Packetdata travels in packets on a computer network.

OSI The interconnection of open systems in accordance with standards of the International

SynchronousA type of two-way communication with virtually no time delay, allowing participants to respond in real time. Also, a system in which regularly occurring events in timed intervals are kept in step using some form of electronic clocking mechanism. (See Asynchronous)

URLClass URL represents a Uniform Resource Locator, a pointer to a "resource"…The syntax of URL is defined by RFC 2396: Uniform Resource Identifiers (URI):…

j

VulnerabilityHardware, firmware, or software flow that leaves an AIS open for potential Organization for Standardization (ISO) for the exchange of information.

Virus exploitation. A weakness in automated system security procedures, administrative controls, physical layout, internal controls, and so forth, that could be exploited by a threat to gain unauthorized access to information or disrupt critical processing.

System a group of independent but interrelated elements comprising a unified whole; "a vast system of **production** and distribution and consumption keep the country going"

SpywareAny software that covertly gathers user information through the user's Internet connection without his or her knowledge, usually for advertising purposes. Spyware applications are typically bundled as a hidden component of freeware or shareware programs that can be downloaded from the Internet. Once installed, the spyware monitors user activity on the Internet and transmits that information in the background to someone else...

Trojan horse an apparently useful and innocent program containing additional hidden code which allows the unauthorized collection, exploitation, falsification, or destruction of data.

TCPSummary: TCP and IP were developed by a Department of Defense (DOD) research...

As with all other communications protocol, TCP/IP is composed of layers:...

978-0-595-38624-6
0-595-38624-5

www.ingramcontent.com/pod-product-compliance
Lightning Source LLC
Chambersburg PA
CBHW051215050326
40689CB00008B/1322